published by

Logan's Dream Publishing Company

©2018

ISBN 978-0692170007

Printed in the United States of America.

This book is dedicated to
my loving family
and
all the teachers and staff
at Wentworth Elementary School
that have inspired and encouraged me
to follow my dreams.
I can never
thank all of you enough.

First, I feel a little wet thing around me.

Then, I crack it open.

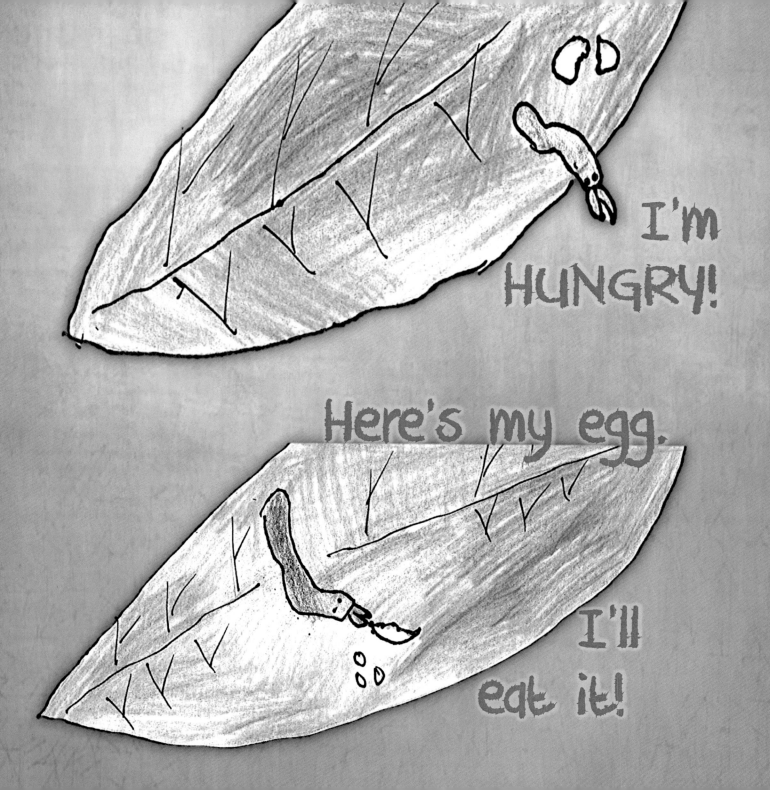

I am not hungry

any more.

I climb back up the tree.

Hook, attach and land.

Now I'm shedding my fourth skin and going up. WOW, my new skin is hard!!

Hold up a minute. This isn't skin, it's a shell! This is cozy. Another day complete!

Good Morning,
I said to myself
the next morning.
I was still in my shell,
but it was a little bit tighter.
WAIT,
it wasn't getting tighter,
I was growing!

But, unusual parts!

Wings, something
growing out of my mouth
and coming out of my head!!
What is happening to me?
Is this a dream,
a trick or what?

My wings are wet so I can't move off of this leaf.

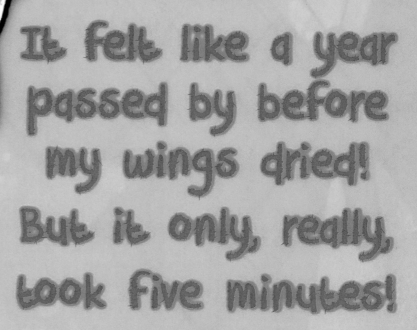

What a shame! It felt like a year passed by before my wings dried! But it only, really, took five minutes!

My wings took me over to a flower.
Then all of a sudden the thing
that grew out of my mouth
drank the flower nectar!

To my surprise
it tasted delicious!

Wait, the thing that grew out of
my mouth looked like a straw!
Kind of weird if you think about it!
The all timers straw!

I thought it was fun,
so I went around
sucking all the "juice"
up
the
"straw."

The next week passed by.

One day my tummy hurt.
I sat down on a
wooden post.
After a minute I
felt better.

A few days later I went back to the post and my children were there.

They were caterpillars, but I could tell they were my precious babies!

The End.

About The Author

Logan is seven years old and has a love of reading and writing.
She began reading before she started Kindergarten and has been reading
Chapter Books like *Black Beauty, Anne of Avonlea* and *Anne of Green Gables* since she was six.
She wants to be a veterinarian and author when she grows up.
Her short-term goal is to have three books published by the time she turns 10-years-old.

Made in the USA
Lexington, KY
02 September 2018